C. Hankins has always loved reading and writing. Throughout her schooling years, she struggled with writing, and her English tutors would point this out to her. Still, that did not stop her from making up stories and writing them at home, especially at a younger age. She felt more at ease because she was not being criticised or judged by the structure/grammar.

At the age of 9 or 10, her love for writing in her diary began, and most evenings, she would reflect on her day and write about it. Hankins loved recounting and sharing her thoughts, sometimes expressing what she couldn't convey to others in writing. As she grew older, she also fell in love with journaling and writing about everything: songs, poems, words of encouragement, testimonies/gratitude, and so forth. Once she starts writing about things, it can be endless, spending hours doing so. It's a desire and passion that has permanently been embedded within her soul; that she finds hard to explain.

Although born in Sierra Leone, Hankins' home is still in the UK, where she has spent most of her life growing up. She loves travelling, and she is blessed to be in a profession that does not limit her but enhances her passion further.

I dedicate this book to my cherished sister, Ann-Marie. Although the choice was never yours when it came to whom your father could be or how your early stage of building blocks was laid down, yet still, your worth and value are far more precious than what the physical eyes may see or behold. You are chosen, loved, and begotten. You are His, the One and True Only!

To the estranged fathers, may your eyes be open to getting a preview and snapshot of each choice being laid down by you. The fatherless, may you always know you are never alone but are forever surrounded by others who may be worthy of taking on the role you desire. Finally, to the fathers who reflect the true heart and description of the Heavenly Father, may you never stop burning that flame for all to witness and bestow.

C. Hankins

In My Father's Arms

Austin Macauley Publishers™
London • Cambridge • New York • Sharjah

The story, experiences, and words are the author's alone.

A CIP catalogue record for this title is available from the British Library.

ISBN 9781398472853 (Paperback)
ISBN 9781398472877 (ePub e-book)
ISBN 9781398472860 (Audiobook)

www.austinmacauley.com

First Published 2022
Austin Macauley Publishers Ltd®
1 Canada Square
Canary Wharf
London
E14 5AA

I would first and foremost like to acknowledge my nephew, Samuel, my nieces, Mary-Ann and Elizabeth, Amechi Odeleye, Nafisa Salisu, Adrienne M Waller, and Taryn Wilkinson. Thank you for your beautiful contributions and for walking this journey with me as you placed your jigsaw piece into this new picture. As always, my dearest mother, Rachel Europa, thank you for always being my pillar of encouragement and strength in the harsh drought of life. Austin Macauley Publishers, you have done it again. Thank you for seeing the vision of my heart and working patiently with me to make the publishing of this new book an enjoyable and rewarding experience.

Table of Contents

Introduction

When we examine the usage of our arms, we can agree that the possibilities are endless from leading, guiding, protecting, comforting, showing assurance, and even more. To be found in the arms of anyone is to be led, guided, protected, comforted, assured, and so forth. What more in the arms of a father? A father is considered to be another who has begotten a child. But in the current generation, we live in, that may not necessarily be the only truth. Others may classify someone else as a father as long as they fulfil any of the above aspects. Pause and think? What do you consider a father, or should I even say, whom do you consider a father? As you read this book, may the clarity of your original perception be made more explicit in your lens or defined in your thinking.

Many believers in Christ pass through their Christian journey and come to a place of realisation that God's intention of an earthly father should mirror His heart as a Heavenly Father. Nonetheless, their journey or account of their memories has left them with a mark of endless questions. The question is if this reality is indeed a desire or an absence of truth from afar.

This book is not like any you may have come across; instead, it zooms in on hidden realities that many may face daily. It keys into the lives of different individuals and their accounts of what they perceive a father to be – simultaneously scooping through their real-life experiences and their memories and thoughts on the whole idea of a father. In so doing, we might be able to see a glimpse from our Heavenly Father's perspective.

Chapter 1
Memory a Mist
(Inspired by a true recount)

We are all faced with different memories of the past. Some memories have helped us shape our lives on how we perceive various matters we may face daily. In contrast, other memories have tainted a mist, which leaves us pondering daily, trying to reach our deepest thoughts when wondering exactly about our understanding of what the memories meant.

Below is a recount of Annie's memory of her experience with an absent father and her thoughts based on the type of picture she has of a father figure.

"A father is someone who is very protective. Someone who provides. Someone who teaches a child about life, which will help them. Someone who nurtures a child, and this will help them to grow into adulthood – someone who is there for them emotionally as well as financially. More so emotionally, since the emotional well-being of a child is paramount. A father is someone a child can look up to as a role model. To inspire the child to become something or even play a part in becoming something.

Growing up, I have always had a missing rib since I didn't know my father. I was informed my father didn't want me and

I was a mistake. My supposed father abandoned me. I had an absence in my life up to the age of thirteen, and then I had the first glimpse of a father figure (my stepdad). It was all a lie since the truth was tainted in this matter, as my experience with my stepdad was not great. Having an absence of a father was normal to me, but when it changed at the age of thirteen, it was not customary for me. The relationship was not good as I had reservations about him and vice versa as he did not know me. We were trying to build up this relationship which never happened until later on in my adulthood. We tried to have this relationship which still never happened as there was so much that had happened that did not allow it to grow."

"Growing up and having a father a mist or even saying having an absent father due to him abandoning me and not being around, (likewise being told somebody did not want me) affected my relationship with men and with trusting them. I find it very difficult to bond with a male in general, especially with strangers. For any male figure in general, there is always something that makes me think they are not good. When I was younger, this particular man (who was a teacher) always passed by our house to go to the school near us. Then somebody pointed him out one day, saying, 'That is your biological father.' Reflecting, I felt so angry inside because I would see this man passing by daily by the road we used to live by as a child. As a person, I never really understood how someone could walk past, knowing where I live but never coming to say hello to me. It brought a lot of questions to my mind which stayed with me. Like how you could be aware of my existence but still not be interested? After questioning my thoughts, I eventually let them go, which affected my mind on men's intentions, even those I had previously dated. I cannot even categorise them but find them to be liars, no good, and I have not yet met any man in my life who has changed my perception. All the ones I have met so far have validated my thoughts about them; they are all the same creatures, reminding me of my father – some of them are deceitful, liars, traitors, and other things. Growing up, I have also witnessed how men treated others, even among my family members, relatives, neighbours, and so forth. I have seen them cheat, lie and treat others around them so badly. So, where do you start? What man can you trust?"

"It is crucial to have both parents; a father and a mother should be present in a child's life while growing up (based on my own experience). It makes a difference in a child's development. Growing up and having that foundation broken from a young age can significantly impact a child's emotions and influence their relationship. The journey for them to recover can be very hard."

(A recount from Annie, who grew up without her biological father. She shared her perception of a father and her memory, which may seem a mist, but on some days, they are as clear as a reflective mirror that highlights what is genuinely staring at them).

There is a need for the genuine Love of a father that protects. An absence of a father can cause anyone to be vulnerable to others or even themselves and lack trust. Those who have experienced this situation or are experiencing the abandonment of a father (or even a father figure) might truly understand the depth and identify with this aspect. However, it may not be the case for everyone.

When faced with years of yearning for someone who had chosen to make themselves a midst, your desire for him can cause a deep sensation of seeking love in the wrong places to fulfil the emptiness that whispers you are not enough.

Maybe you have walked this journey of abandonment or awakening the reality of what you are currently experiencing. I want to reassure you that you are not alone! This journey does not need to be battled alone. There is a father that seeks to shower you to experience no other.

In my Father's arm, you find Love, not the Love that the world systems confuse you with, but the pure Love, the Love that keeps on believing in you even if you have stopped believing in yourself. The Love that sees the best in you, the Love that was shown by the act He did when He gave His only begotten Son up so that you can be reconciled back into His arm. Giving you His best and precious gifts and desiring for you to receive them.

John 3 vs 16 NIV (New International Version) Bible
"For God so loved the world that He gave His one and only Son, that whoever believes in Him shall not perish but have eternal life."

Forgiveness

As we walk this road called life,
We are faced with daily opportunities that will require us to demonstrate Forgiveness.
Although quickly said it's harder to practice.
Forgiveness exposes you to be vulnerable to the offender.
When hurt, every part of your being shouts revenge,
Revenge to punish the offender,
Or even a physical infliction to temporarily take your hurt away.
Still, the matter of truth is,
The hurt is not dealt with,
It's only temporary.
When you don't forgive, you become a prisoner in a cell of hurt.
Locked away to rot with no access out.
The anchor to Forgiveness is Love.
Love is a key to unlocking the prison cell of unforgiveness so that you are confident to walk in the freedom of Forgiveness.
This key of Love is not like any other.
It requires you to go to the Locksmith for Him to design the specific key for the cell.
The Locksmith understands each cell, its roots, and what key will suit it.

He directs you on how the key should be turned to release the cell door without further damage.

We all have access to the Locksmith if we only follow the path He has laid for us.

He first demonstrated the freedom of Forgiveness for us to follow.

God, who is our Locksmith, is always available.

If only we would humble ourselves to admit we are in a cell that needs His key for release.

He understands how easily you can be locked up in that cell.

Strive to steer away from it.

Still, due to human nature,

This can be a challenge.

Nevertheless, always remember Love,

Which can settle the impossible,

And prevent you from human nature that easily entangles us to walk the path that leads to the cell of unforgiveness.

So choose daily to walk in the path of Love.

In order to demonstrate the richness of Forgiveness

For all those who may cross your path.

Chapter 2
Gone but Not Forgotten

(Inspired by a true recount)

Have you ever wondered about the possibilities of things or even found yourself asking the question of 'What if?' Yet still, you might not have even asked 'What if' but rather pondered what could have been... Things or people who are valuable to us will always have a lasting impact even if they are no longer there. If we could, we would forever hold on to what we love and value. But forever is not in our own hands or capacity. Can we ever blur our memories of those that meant a lot to us even after they are no longer there? We can all share our thoughts on this depending on the zooming angle or the experience we encountered.

"If someone was to say the word 'father' to me, the image which springs to my mind will be my dad opening a door, bringing me breakfast, doing my nails/hair, or playing outside. It will be of him doing something for me because that's what he did. He showed me that I was worthy. That I deserved to be treated a certain way. Sometimes the images can be him telling me, 'You're so beautiful', and showing his love for me. From the act he did and demonstrated towards me, I saw him as a leader, a supporter, someone who loved me unconditionally, kind of like a hero when I ponder what he meant to me. Leader because he was leading the family by setting that example, especially for us. I was a daddy's girl. He was my champion! The simplest of things he would do. Since I had both a dad and a father, I tend to use the word 'dad' for him, as that's what he was to me, a biological father. My dad filled that role and stood in my life. He was always there. Whatever I was doing, I was amazing. To him, I was great. One time, I could remember coming down the stairs with my sweatpants, and he said to me, 'You look really nice today.' I was like, 'Daddy, I don't look nice. I'm in sweatpants; what are you talking about?' When I really dressed up, he made a big deal out of it. But he also used to joke. When my mom used to press my hair, he would make sound effects as a joke. Part of why I called him a hero was because when he died, it exemplified this idea. The pet store sent him a floral arrangement even though he didn't know the people. But he had this presence that everyone was a friend everywhere he went. Everybody was part of his community, even if he had never seen them before. I remembered being at the grocery store, and he greeted this particular lady and asked about her family. I also remembered thinking and asking him how he knew all these people and their families. He responded that he didn't know them or their family, but he was certain that everyone has to have a family, and everybody cares about their family. Therefore, he could ask anyone about their family, and I should do it too. In terms of a hero, I was not saying he was perfect because my dad had flaws. But he would always put forth his best. I mean, that's what heroes do! They show up for everybody, try, and support wherever they need while always giving their best. Reflecting on my fond, happy, tearful memories, which I know I won't have again of him, was when I used to live in Chicago; most mornings, I would talk to him as I rode to work. He was always so encouraging and would ask me, 'What's today going to be like, sweetheart? What's today going to be like, princess?' And if I responded with something negative like 'I'm not looking forward to today because of this…', he'd have a response for me opposite of my negativity. He would always say just before he would get off the phone, for me to have a good day, and if I didn't, then it's my fault. Mind you, I never understood what he meant, and I used to be irritated and respond to him like, 'No, this could happen, or somebody could do this.' However, when he died, I finally understood what he had meant. My dad was right. You cannot control anybody else, but you can control yourself. You can control how you respond to situations or others or even how things impact you. So you having a good day is completely a choice. It doesn't matter what hits you. Still, in the midst of that, some situations may impact you greatly, like his death. Nonetheless, in general, you have a choice to decide what today is going to be like or the words you may even speak over today. What might be simple and basic phone calls to others are my fondest memories that have marked my heart forever. Whenever he pops into my mind, I still have the image of him always being kind. Compassion was always flowing out of him like a stream of a river. Also, the ability to care and bring joy to others while making them smile in many ways others don't. It was honestly so beautiful to witness. My father was not just my father but a dad to a lot of people. What he was in people's lives, he was like sunshine on a cloudy day. A lot of people don't even get one great father. This bond still exists even though he hadn't born me and didn't come into my life until I was five. I know what a gift and blessing it was to have him in my life. Indeed, he was important to me. Grief doesn't end but changes and looks different as the years fade away. There are more disappointments of what I won't get because he is not here anymore. If anyone were to ever go through what I had of losing a father/dad so dear to them or even someone going through a similar situation, I would encourage them never to forget such a jewel. They don't need to worry about it. Rather, hold and live their greatness through their lives. Always embody their spirit your way and in a way that all the things you remember about their greatness and awesomeness will be a light for others in the world."

(A. Waller's recount: World-Wide Educator)

Amid sorrow, trying to see the drips and drops of being hopeful can leave you doubtful while struggling to get by each day. Regardless of this… Remaining **HOPEFUL** as you:

Hold
Onto
Precious
mom**E**nts
Forever
Unchangeable
Love

For those who have gone before us, their presence will live in our hearts ALWAYS!

Chapter 3
Present but Nowhere to Be Found

(Inspired by a true recount)

Although no one can see the wind, they are confident it's there. The softness and harshness of brushing or beating against your skin can make you sure of its presence. Likewise, there are fathers of their existence in your life you question deeply. These fathers may demonstrate your need for their presence during the different seasons of your life but can also leave you pondering how much of their existence they have freely given you and are not withholding from you.

Some children are currently experiencing their fathers, who may be present on some occasions and absent daily – questioning if they are anywhere to be found. Below is an account of three children whose words echo their everyday experiences.

"Loving, caring, and patient are the words that stick out to us when we think of our father. A father is meant to love you, care for you and be patient with you no matter what. Even when you are angry with them, they are meant to be patient until you are no longer angry. Growing up and not currently living with our father can be hard. He does take care of us and puts us before himself. More so, he helps people when they need help. Especially when we need his help, he always says 'yes.' Whenever our father can, he will take us out, and when asked for something, he does get it. Still, not having him always around is not so great. You can have your mum and dad together and suddenly be missing one. It makes you question, who do you love more? Or sometimes, you love them the same but can be confused. When you see him, the timing of when you will see him is not great, and it can be saddening when pondering over whether not to invite him to important events. Growing up now is not so great with his absence. It just isn't the same not to have him always around. It's sad not to have both parents to take care of you. When one parent is missing, it is like having one part of your heart missing. We miss our father being around to take care of us and to help us when we are sad or lonely."

(A recount from three precious little souls)

Have you ever felt this way, or are you even feeling like this? Having one parent currently not present in your home, especially a father can create a missing piece within you. Yes, your excitement shoots up 100% when you visit or spend time with him. Yet, that reversely changes to 1% when he is not there. Lying there at night wondering about the possibility of 'If only he were around... just maybe, maybe, things may look, feel or be different.' Maybe this could be the case, or maybe even not. No one truly knows. But those questions that beat against your mind from time to time or even daily are not necessarily wrong. Condemning or feeling guilty for those questions can be wrong. Many of you in this position need 'assurance.' Assurance that even though your father is usually nowhere to be found, it doesn't mean you are alone. I know, right? Easier said than experienced. There is a Heavenly Father who is always there. His presence is never absent. It illuminates brighter than the bright sun. He doesn't obstruct or brings denial to your earthly father's absence but rather gives you that confidence of 'He Has You!' His full expression of love, care, and patience is not limited only to when you acknowledge His existence but, in the stillness, when no one is around. In your Father's arms, there is assurance. Assurance that He is there through every storm and joy. Each journey of life is not limited to how much of Himself you can have. He wants to pour His fullness and genuinely experience being in His arms.

Always
Stand
Secure
Under
Real
Abundance
Never
Ceasing
Eternal (lov**E**, hop**E**, grac**E**)

Chapter 4
Almost Replaceable

(Inspired by a true recount)

What was your favourite toy or object while growing up? What was so special about that particular thing? That specific thing or toy was probably so precious to you. Should in case anything has happened to it, it would have left you in a place of despairs. You could have probably gone to any extent to make sure it was safe and sound, making others around you also see its worth and value as much as you did. We all find ourselves in situations that we wouldn't necessarily have picked if we were to be given the same chance again. Still, greater joy can arise during an unlikely crisis if only we are open to witnessing and partaking in what it brings.

"When someone says Father to me, it automatically means God. Honestly, that's all I see as God is my Father, He is my everything, He is the one that gave me life, that helps me get through the day and the years. So Father is God to me. That's what my heart says. But at the same time, in this world and day and age, meaning a father figure that you live with as a child growing up. These are the two points that come to my mind when I hear the word 'father.' I do believe there is a big difference between the word 'father' and the word 'dad.' I feel like there is more of a deeper connection with the word 'father' than the word 'dad'. With 'father', I know I cannot disrespect my father, and even if I were to do so, it would not be intentional. I feel 'dad' is a bit more lenient and free. Being a foster child and growing up without a biological family, I ended up building and creating a good dad-and-daughter relationship with my foster dad, which was rewarding and a blessing to experience. But having God as my father, that relationship was always there, and I just had to acknowledge and accept it as I walked in it. My experience growing up as a child without a biological father was difficult. There were times when I just wanted to speak to my father, see him, and really wanted to get to know him. It was hard growing up and not seeing the two people who gave birth to you. I vaguely remembered speaking to him once in a while. Still, only God knows if it was him I was speaking to or another person. Growing up in foster care, I got social service to help me locate my father because I wanted the opportunity to develop a relationship. They could find and locate him in Africa, and he wasn't currently in the country. When we were going to make the first call to talk to him, I remembered the goosebumps emerging on my arms due to nerves (and being only ten years old). Although the joy was there before making that call, I didn't know how to feel after the number was dialled and I heard his voice. I wouldn't say it was a good experience speaking to him, but, reflecting, it was an experience I could remember. We spoke a couple more times, and the bonus of all was that my foster dad was the one that contributed to finding my biological dad and making those phone calls possible. He understood the importance of finding a member of your family and speaking and having a connection with them. He even made it an effort to travel to Africa to meet him on my behalf, took photos of him, and brought them back to me. The act of what he did truly made me admire the extent he took as a foster dad. After speaking to my biological father several times, things didn't go as planned. The whole picture I had built in my mind of the father and daughter fairy-tale reunion of me jumping into his arms and him just holding me wasn't what happened. It got to a point where I didn't want to speak to him anymore but began to see my foster dad as more of a dad in all the effort he was making to contribute to my growing up. Whenever we went to restaurants or spoke to others, he would always acknowledge me as his daughter. When we moved to a new town and were racially bullied in school, he went there and protected me as his daughter. I was so amazed that he still had my back despite the colour barrier and wanted to protect me as his own. I had different countless childhood experiences with him, and he worked so hard to get the unspoken medal as a father even though he didn't have to, but I truly respect him for doing so."

(*Nafisa's story, fostered from a young age*)

We may not choose biological parents, but we can choose those who lead and guide us in this life journey. Daily we awake to choices from all angles, and we will have to decide which road to choose. Being young, many can rely on parents with the sole responsibility to lead and guide them on the right path. Still, when those who have been given the sole responsibility are amidst our lives, does it make life standstill? If only you look around, you may be able to identify the beauty from your ashes and see the alternate people who have been empowered to lead and guide you. Yes, they may not have been the first choice, but they still could be the best final choice. Suppose you have gone through having a father vanish could relate to the yearning of why. But remember the others God placed around you. Know they were the chosen replaceable of what was before and the best choice for you now.

Chapter 5
The Ideal Perception

(Inspired by a true recount)

Some say our eyes are the gateway to our soul. How much of that statement is true, I sincerely do not know. If anyone was to ask me where I heard such information from, I ultimately could not tell you where I first heard it. Still, it sounds very catchy, doesn't it? It's probably a saying you might accidentally say in an unexpected situation (if it is related). Or maybe not; who knows? In most circumstances, all you can honestly state is anything related to what you can perceive. Your perception will always seem right in your sight since it's mainly based on your experiences. Should anyone argue it wrong, it might inflict some wounds. Wounds you will want to shield to the best of your ability. We all have an ideal perception of different aspects of our lives and, what's more, a perfect perception of a father. Whether or not that perception is reality, it doesn't matter to some. Instead, we prefer it to merge into the perfect picture we would like to paint, which each individual is entitled to (no matter what others may echo out from their heart).

"The word 'father' brings about safety and protection in my mind. It automatically means God as my mind just went straight there. Still, my fond memory of growing up as a little girl is my relationship with my biological dad. Being able to sit on his lap, lay against him, or be affectionately at ease with him welcoming it; without anything funny. I know it will be a weird thing in today's society, especially greeting or saying goodbye to a father by kissing him. Yet still, this was the kind of connection I had with my dad as a child. Although there were other fond memories, this was the one that stuck out to me. Concerning not-so-good memories, I can think of two major things which came to mind. One is when he went through a spot change of depression (a kind of change of life), and he started drinking, which affected us significantly. I mean, he never really liked alcohol even though he used to have a cider frequently in the past, yet still, it was never a hectic thing. But through the change of life period, when he was so depressed, he started drinking more and tried to hide it, which affected us quite deeply and resulted in family counselling. It even got to a place when my mom made an alternate. If he were not going to change or sort himself out, then there would be an alternate of my mom making a final decision that no one wanted as it messed things for us as a family. His actions caused our world to be rocked a bit. Likewise, reflecting on the car journeys with him, he used to be very wild. He always wanted to prove a point. That pride and eagerness that comes before a fall. Once, he tried to stand up to another guy and beat him up in front of my sister and me (because he wanted to prove a point). This situation left us kind of traumatised and nagged us up to this present day. It's not a joy to ride with him. To us, it just spoke volumes of, do you love us? Is wanting to prove a point to someone else more important than our safety and well-being? These are the questions that replay in my mind. Road rage is a thing we faced from this experience. Especially where I am from, people can even involve guns and leave others' lives in danger. Therefore, all those things came to play in my mind and made me question if his heart was towards me. There is and isn't a difference between those who grow up with and without a father. It's a yes and no answer. Just because a father is present doesn't mean he is being the daddy or fulfilling the role he is meant to fulfil. He can be an absent father or even be there but physically/emotionally abusive and be hurting the family/loved ones in the household. Sometimes, having him around doesn't necessarily mean it's better. It all comes down to the individual being in a healthy and emotional state of mind. If a father does not deal with his things or issues, they bleed on others. Which, in turn, messes up everyone else's lives and world. Therefore, it doesn't always make a difference to have a father around if he is not healthy. Yet, if the brokenness and flaws rise to the surface, he must be willing to work on them. The effect might look different for those whose fathers are not around. However, there are negative effects for those whose fathers are around but are not fulfilling their role as they should in a healthy way. Being around, not fulfilling their role, and being absent are both negative effects on the individual as it causes an internal bleed and wound."

(Gee, an expert teacher from the land of 'The Big Five')

Find comfort in the good as well as the bad. Find comfort in the truth, as well as the lie. Find comfort in the plenty and also the lack. Find it in your present circumstance and even the past. Some have, and others don't, and those that have may desire what they don't.

Nonetheless, those that don't have, may desire to have. Walking in a person's shoes is not ideal, but finding comfort in your journey is more realistic. When viewing one's life, where do you place yourself? The present or the past. The ideal or the yearning? Your perception may not be the ideal one for another. Yet still, comfort is extended for the state you have or are in.

Chapter 6
Still Hope

The trials of life can leave us shattered and broken without warnings. No one fully prepares an individual for all they may face in life. Even with uttered words, it cannot paint half the picture of what you see and experience. Once a book is read, you know and expect what the end will be, should, in case it's reread. As the saying goes, you live to learn, or instead, you learn to live. But what happens if tragedy strikes unexpectedly from a young age when learning to live has not yet been established. Take heart; that's when living to learn is taken a toll on the hope that arises each day.

"If someone was to say the word 'father' to me, automatically, the image which springs to my mind will be someone who has a really strong stature. To have such a strong stature will imply protection. Likewise, someone who is tall and massive that can scare people away will be another image. Now the word 'father' means to be a person who protects, just like the image that springs to my mind – a caring, loving, hard-working person who can give direction in their leading."

"Many people may think there is a difference between growing up with a father and those who do not, but how I look at a father figure is different from those of other people, to be honest, and it could honestly be because I grew up without one. At this current moment of my life, if I was to pause and think, it's like looking forward to maybe what could have been. It's hard to think of a memory of my biological father as he died when I was still relatively young, so I find it difficult to even think of what type of a father he was to me."

"The specific depths of the difference between those who grow up with a father and me growing up without one will never be one I will ever know. Nonetheless, I am genuinely aware a father has a role. A family unit without a father is not quite the same as one that has one. Equally, I have been so blessed to have a mother who has gone over and beyond. She has been able to do harvest and fulfil the gap in the absence of a father. Would life have been different if he had been around or was still here? I do not know. It's an answer that can never fully be answered and will always be lingering for eternity to come. This then influences my perspective on how I view what a father is or should look like."

"Raising my own young family, I am now beginning to witness the significance of having a father around at such a young age. As previously mentioned, my father passed away when I was very young, and my eldest child is, by far, younger than I was when I had lost him. Until she gets to that age that I was, I will get to see the role of what I had truly missed out on. Currently, my daughter is getting her love, care, and support from my husband, just like the age I was when I received all those things from my father. As she reaches her early teens or the age I was without his presence, I will most probably see things differently, even how a father disciplines someone he loves or gives direction, support, and nurture. I also witnessed how a home is run, the dynamic of families, and how the father's role plays in the midst of it all; this is something I look forward to. Indeed, my heart does look forward to those missed moments, knowing that the opportunity will sooner than later take place.

"During the growing-up stage of my life, I might have missed out on some things because my mom took on the role of two parents by working, being attentive, and rallying around four other children (my siblings). Yet still, I cannot downplay the God factor and the faith my mother had that encouraged her to give her all to us and be all she could be in the role of being both parents. In the world we live in, many individuals lose their fathers at different stages of their lives. I don't think about these types of people at times as I don't compare myself to them. Still, I am aware that the way we grow up, our lives are affected and shaped by how we have been raised, and the environment, including the people who have raised us and their own life experiences, can influence us too. In my life, maybe I would have been even more afraid to make some of the mistakes I had made when I was a teenager. Definitely, at school, I would have been much more focused and stayed away from the wrong friends. My absence of a father influenced some decisions I have made and how I viewed certain things in life."

"Reflecting, I could state that not being raised by a father may have resulted in me being independent, strong-willed, motivated, and tough. Taking responsibility and dealing with what I had was crucial too. I know those who have both parents may also be facing similar challenges, but when you have to journey through asking or depending on both parents to just having one, there is a shift and change in the way you view or live life and how you may frame your world in the long run. People have different life challenges due to not having a father, like dealing with hurdles and not always being fully equipped with what life may throw."

"My encouragement to those walking this journey I have been on or might walk that road one day is that life is like a jigsaw. As long as you have all the pieces, things will eventually connect, although you may not necessarily know what the final image may look like in the end. Growing up, I had to hold on to my faith and still do so by choice. My faith has helped me on this journey. I see God's hand being there when I lost my father, up until this present moment. I cannot deny the significance of a mom and a dad, and what a shame it might be too loose either. Yet still, it's not all lost. Life does not have to be all doomed and gloomed. Hope can still arise during loss. If you genuinely look closely, you would be able to identify the best people God has placed around you, and sometimes it might just be one person. I discovered although I didn't have one person to call 'dad', I still had many individuals who gave me what I needed at the time of my need which kept my hope burning throughout each season of my life."

(Recount by Ami, devoted wife and mom of two)

Remaining Hopeful:

Many hold on to what they would like to have, even if it never takes place. A world that throws your everything under the sun can leave you in a place of despair as some things you take for yourself would rather exchange for another. Thus far, one instead wonders how you respond in the midst of the unexpected knocking at your front and back door, especially when you are least prepared.

Remaining hopeful when the unexpected happens can never be followed by a manual. If there were one, we would all be the true experts in our lives. Nonetheless, the unforeseen parts of life can leave us self-trained to remain hopeful in a world where hope is dimming by the hour.

Part 2

Chapter 7
Hindrances from His Arms

There are many benefits each of us can utter on the role of those who are significant in our lives and the impact they make. Likewise, many of the believing faith can proclaim how important their belief keeps them going through each stage and season of life. Many people can agree there is a higher being, but only some may proclaim or testify that the higher being is God. The ones that proclaim and testify must have that total confidence that the One True Father is God despite what the majority echoes out. Even from what they may have experienced or are experiencing in this life, they are encouraged to know they have a father who has their back and cares for them deeply, wanting to be part of their life's journey. As profane as it may sound to many, still to the some, or even the few, they are not shaken to think differently. To be in the arms of the One True Father is unexplainable. It doesn't mean your life is perfect because He has your back. Surely not! Instead, you may experience even more than those who do not have Him. But knowing and having that full assurance that He is at your very side – a Father who is with you along each step you take is more valuable than any words you can express.

But if an individual is not careful, many hindrances can prevent them from being in the arms of the One True Father. The hindrances do not present themselves with warning signs, as they are not bad things to any natural eyes. Even though they are not bad things, if one is not careful, it can prevent them from running or being in the arms of direction, protector, provider, and many more the soul requires. Devaluing the significant role of what the father wants to have in your life could leave an individual feeling unsatisfied. These hindrances can be identified in different shapes and forms, such as materialism, families, friends, media, self, and the endless list continues.

Self is a big hindrance that can prevent an individual from being in the arms of the Father, as self only cares and desires to feed its own satisfaction. Self would always want its own way. Many people are occupied with things that involve only themselves. So that they do not spend a lot of time, (if not any) with their heavenly Father. There was a time when I was fixated on trying to sort my life and live it the way I wanted to so that I drifted from the arms of my Father. I would be occupied with travelling from one destination to the other, allowing myself to be so busy that I had no time to spend in the arms of my Father. Planning every stage of my own life was a craving for me that I struggled to allow Him to direct my steps. Most times, I would fight toward where He was leading me. When I had some time, I would enable laziness to come in the way and allow the day to pass by me without captivating myself in His arms, even with the endless invitations received and the deep sensing desire that my soul was clinging for Him. Some may probably relate to being like this, or even you were once like this when you have allowed 'self' to be the directing factor in your life as you have embraced only in the arms of self. To others, maybe this is your current situation, and you might have questioned its normality from time to time. If that is the case, make a choice right now to rise up from self. Allow your heavenly Father to give you the strength that is needed not to put self first. Instead, allow the grace to be sufficient in your life so that you can separate the time that you would have spent solemnly on self to spend in the arms of your Father. The true sacrifice of self is complex and not easily done, but taking the back seat will create room for the True One to let His full manifestation in you.

Family is another hindrance that might prevent you from being in the One True Arms. Do not get me wrong because family is critical and fundamental in one's life. Yet, if there is no balance created and your family takes all your heart, mind, and soul that you do not even have time for others or even a relationship with your Father, then an imbalance is created. Suppose you only allow your family to be the only focus in life and refuse to give time for a relationship to cultivate and grow, blossoming each passing season of time. In that case, there will be an unexplainable need you will seek to fill. Avoiding your Father's arms or allowing each moment to be only for your family can cause you to become drained, leading you to not give your best to them. One thing is, you cannot provide what you do not have, so if you do not receive the fullest of what you are from your Father, you would struggle and find it tiresome to keep on giving your best and pouring out day in and night to your family. Allow Him to be at the centre of your family. Daily learn to receive to the fullest from

Him (as your provider) by immersing yourself in His giving Arms.

Materialism has not just been a hindrance in this present era for individuals to be in the arms of their One True Father, but it has always been an issue since man fell into sin. The dictionary defines it as a tendency to consider material possessions and physical comfort as more important than spiritual values. Those from the believing faith will maybe agree that the explained definition was demonstrated the day Adam and Eve chose to eat the fruit (physical/material possession) over the word of God (spiritual values). From then, many individuals will choose to live their lives with the materials/physical possession of this world rather than live their lives with the spiritual values (that comes from the word of God). The quality of being in your Father's Arms is more important than the quantity of material possessions and physical comfort. Either one way or the other, if individuals are not careful, they can be occupied with the different materialism of this world without realising it. Far be it for me to condemn materialism by stating it is terrible for our lives. But, as soon as your most authentic love is for it and how you can keep on gaining more and more while replacing your valuable time being in the One True Arms, it becomes a hindrance. You set yourself on a mousetrap, always chasing and wanting more but never being fully satisfied, as it becomes the idol of your daily living and everything you strive for.

The beauty of the right friends you bond with purely to be part of your life's story is an authentic, admirable gift for anyone to have. Friends are very important in life, and without having at least that one genuine person, the rest can prevent you from being in the Arms of the Father or even lead you on the wrong path. The bible declares that Jesus had twelve disciples who were considered to be His friend. Conversely, among the twelve, one was his betrayer, and there was dynamic amongst the others. Not every friend who comes your way is true towards your path of life's journey, as some can bring or be a hindrance, especially if the season in your life is way overdue. A true friend chooses to love you and desires nothing but the best for you at all times, regardless of the ups and downs and changes in season you may face or experience together. That friend may not necessarily be in agreement with you, but their heart of gold always radiates the truth with gentle love that penetrates to the core of the person you desire to become daily. With such a friend, they may have a glimpse of understanding the fundamental role of your Father and will always desire your relationship with Him to continue and take its form. Be careful but not afraid to have the right influence of friends in your life, praying and hoping the wrong types will be sieved from being a hindrance, and the right friends will draw you nearer to always being in His arm as you always replicate the sincere value of love you have for them.

As long as there is a breath in your lungs, blood pumping throughout your veins, and you are living in this present era, you are most probably being affected by the media one way or the other. The media significantly impacts how individuals live their lives and what they should or shouldn't be doing. To say the damaging effect of this to many individuals is understated. To a believer of the faith, you are challenged daily on how your life should be directed and hear constant criticising your faith and how it should look like even though those same people that dictate will not be found near the actual Truth. You want and desire only the Father to lead you, yet man battles for his place in your life while also bringing the full judgement. Once again, don't get me wrong, as there are many benefiting factors to the media.

Nonetheless, when you allow your life to be governed and dictated by everything the media states, you gradually become vulnerable to failure and not living or being the fullest in what your Father has called you to on this earth. Knowing that He has created you and has a divine purpose for your life with a manual on the best way to operate here on this earth always brings comfort. Identifying yourself in this aspect doesn't defeat you. Being willing to change today and allowing forgiveness to shift your perspective of what truly matters is essential in the Arms of Your Father.

Hindrances may even present themselves to be more than what has been said above. Being in constant communion with Him will cause praise to arise even amid troubles. No matter how bleak or hopeless life might be or even in the most joyous moments of your life, strive not to allow those times to be a hindrance that separates you further from His loving Arms. Instead, let your striving be meaningful as you are found in the Arms of the One True Father.

Broken Chains:

When you are in chains, you are restricted with your movements and paralysed from one area to another. Chains are used for those who are captured and need to be held in bondage. Mankind was in chains when Adam and Eve fell into temptation in the Garden of Eden, leading mankind to be captured by sin!

Chains became existence when man sinned and was therefore driven out of Eden. That day, not only was man physically banished from his surrounding, but they were spiritually in chains and no longer in freedom.

Centuries after centuries, mankind remained in chains, and many were paralysed physically as well as spiritually towards achieving their full potential or God-given destiny in this world.

However, all hope was not lost. Before the existence of time itself, God had ordained redemption for all mankind. Although man, from creation, could not yet see what was ahead, but God Almighty could foresee what was yet to come. One glorious night, a Saviour was born! Angels rejoiced to know that man's freedom has come into existence to bestow and break the chains placed on man from creation.

Three years in ministry and the Redeemer spent time restoring the physical paralysed and proclaiming the Good News. Hope for complete Redemption by the Redeemer became fully established when the Saviour of the world was placed on the cross. He completed the redemption as He spoke, 'It is finished!' No longer a glorious night but a glorious day of man's chains being forever broken through Him. Being physically or spiritually paralysed no longer has authority since the curtains were torn in the middle to show that man can return to his Creator and be restored from broken chains!

Chapter 8
Rest in His Arms

In a world that is filled with many weary souls, many yearn to rest. Rest from a busy day at work, rest from coursework, exams, endless studying, or even the demands of giving your all to everyone but yourself. Many lay in bed at night but are still wide awake in their minds as time flickers the night away. No matter how much they toss and turn, they struggle to rest their weary souls and tiresome minds. The soul yearns for rest but still struggles to find it when searching in the wrong places. When an individual is sick, they need prescribed medicine from a doctor. Likewise, when someone needs to learn, they seek a teacher/trainer to teach them. Self-diagnosis or self-taught might not target the actual need of the issue like a specific specialised individual. There is One that knocks daily in the heart of the weary soul. One who is not seen in the physical eye but the spiritual. He stands and knocks, patiently waiting for you to open and find rest in His Arms. The question is presented daily: would you open for Him?

Resting in His arms can and may look different to each person who opens the door for Him to enter. Just like each relationship you have is different in its unique way, so also it's true when it comes to resting in His Arms. It will look different to others, or even yourself, during the different seasons of life.

To some, they may desire to be close from a distance, and to others, closeness is one to be pursued on a daily basis as it brings beauty to others who want it. In His presence, in constant communion, the reflection of the beauty begins.

A cultivated relationship will take its actual forming in the journey you embark on, and it may also prove how genuine it is or if it was ever there to begin with.

The relationship is continuous through each season of life. Not only do you need to know this but also believe. You can know something, but it might only take its full effect when you actually believe it to be true and to the fullest. Therefore, it's not only knowing that the relationship is there for others but also believing it is there for you as well.

Choosing to accept a relationship with God is a starting point for you to rest in His Arms as the door of your heart is open for Him to enter.

Acceptance in Christ.

As individuals, we spend most of our lives, if not all, comparing ourselves with other individuals. A bad habit and mindset to have but, unfortunately, becomes the norm every day. It can hinder you from reaching that destination God has in store for you because you are occupied walking in someone else's shoes and path. Life is not intended to be so! In the bible, we identify that God is not a respecter of man. So why do you only become a respecter of man's voice instead of God? The world system has normalised that what people think or say about you is important, pressuring individuals to believe specific images about their lives and how they should live.

In Christ, you find true acceptance. His voice is the one that should echo past all other voices. You don't need to force yourself to be like anybody else. Just Be You, the person you have been created to be in your unique self. He sees the best in you when others see the worse – picking you up when the demanding, broken world tries to crush you down. He is always giving you hope and joy when fear tries to grip your heart. Learn daily to accept yourself in Christ when you are resting in His Arms.

Who has never experienced resting in His Arms? The Father of all fathers wants to draw you nearer. You do not have to go searching for other alternatives of satisfaction in the world or someone else's arms. Although you may find them, but they are temporary and will always fade away without a warning. True fulfilment will never be established from temporary things. No matter how much you press on, it will surely not last long. Knowing the One True Father is essential. With the heart of knowing Him daily, you also begin to discover your most authentic self. You do not have to spend another day not resting in Him. To experience life like no other, CHOOSE today to run straight and find rest in the arms like no other. The One True Father.

Conclusion

In My Father's Arms: when all is said and done

No one's life story is ever summed up in just one moment. Neither can the ideal of a father be stated into one category. No matter how similar an experience may be, the way we respond to it may be different. Each of us has an idea of a father based on what we have been told, read, or might have experienced. Some are currently experiencing a father's role as you navigate through your life's journey.

At times, the expectations which we could have of them can slip through the cracks. We forget, as people, that no one is perfect. Although there are responsibilities that we all have, we quickly falter when trying to fulfil them. In that manner, no father is perfect, just like no one on earth is perfect. Many fathers have experienced their own life journey beyond what they may share or utter to any soul. Their experience has contributed and often influences them as they try to make sense of each step they take. To some, the impact has been more so than others.

As long as we remain human beings, there will always be some imperfections. But, we must decide if we are willing to accept and see past the shortcomings of the fathers in our lives (whoever and wherever they may be)?

There is always GRACE that abounds. Learn to be gracious as you love the fathers in your life. Whether they are yours or have stepped into the role, know that them learning to be what you desire is an ongoing process throughout this life journey.

There is One Person who far exceeds any expectations we may ever have of a father. He models the ideal perception of a father and wants to be active as you live each day. It takes your acceptance of Him. An open heart of approval and a step out knowing He has you in the very palm of His arms, no matter what life itself may say or bring your way. Are you willing to say YES to Him? The choice is yours: to be in the arms of not just any father but The Father – forever knowing; that in His divine arms, there will always be a heart of LOVE that pours out Forgiveness, Protection, Comfort, Assurance, Guidance, and Hope.

"And I give them eternal life, and they shall never perish; neither shall anyone snatch them out of My hand. My Father, who has given them to Me, is greater than all; and no one is able to snatch them out of My Father's hand. I and My Father are one." (John 10:28–30 NKJV)